TABLE OF CONTENTS

—————◆◇◆—————

The Secret of
　　Your Future
Is Hidden In
　　Your Daily
Routine.

-MIKE MURDOCK

THE GREATEST SUCCESS HABIT ON EARTH

Habit Is A Gift From God.

Too often when someone thinks of the word habit, we think of *bad* habits, such as smoking, drinking and taking drugs.

Habit simply means that anything you do twice becomes easier. You can create *good* habits just as you can begin wrong habits.

Great Men Have Great Habits

Jesus had a habit of attending worship services. He went into the synagogue on the Sabbath day and stood up to read. "And He came to Nazareth, where He had been brought up: and, *as His custom was,* He went into the synagogue on the sabbath day, and stood up for to read," (Luke 4:16).

The Psalmist prayed 7 times a day. "Seven times a day do I praise Thee because of Thy righteous judgments," (Psalm 119:164).

Daniel had a habit of praying 3 times each day. "He kneeled upon his knees three times a day, and prayed, and gave thanks before his God, as he did aforetime," (Daniel 6:10).

The difference in champions is their *habits*.

- ▶ Champions Do Daily What Losers Are Only Willing To Do Occasionally.
- ▶ The Secret To Your Future Is Hidden In Your Daily Routine.
- ▶ What You Do Daily Determines What You Will Become Permanently.
- ▶ Your Success In Life Is Determined By The Habits You Develop.

That is why I listen to the Scriptures on cassette every morning when I first awaken. That is why I read the Bible consistently. You see, the Bible is like a mirror that reveals the truth about me and my relationship with God. Every Word is an eternal *Seed planted* in the soil of my mind.

Reading The Word of God Daily Is The Greatest Success Habit On Earth.

2

EACH WORD GOD SPEAKS IS LIKE A SEED PLANTED IN THE SOIL OF YOUR MIND

Your Mind Grows Any Thought That Enters It.

Your Mind Is Like Soil. It will *grow* any Seed you place in it...*good* or *bad*. It will not differentiate or discriminate. If you sow wrong Seeds into the soil, it will grow a wrong Harvest. Sowing good Seeds *grows* good Harvests.

Years ago someone tested children in two separate rooms where toys and dolls were. In the first room they showed a video tape of someone *stomping* on the heads of dolls. The children in that room who watched the video, picked up the dolls and began to stomp them...*exactly as they had seen on the video.*

On the video in the second room, the dolls were picked up and stroked and loved. The children who saw that video...*began to stroke the dolls!* They did what they saw.

What You Continually See, You Will Eventually Do.

That's why the Bible should become the Master Mentorship Program in your home. It is a *Collection of Photographs*...planted like Seeds in your subconscious mind.

Pictures of *Rewards* for those who fear God. Pictures of Pain for those disobedient and defiant to God.

Think of the picture of the prodigal son in the pig pen. That Seed-Picture reveals the eventuality of every child who disrespects the authority of their home. It also is a picture of restoration to those willing to repent and return home to the arms of a merciful father.

Think of the prophet's words to the widow of Zarephath. Her offering unleashed her financial provision throughout the entire famine. The Rewards of Obedience are pictures that birth a holy desire to embrace even illogical instructions from men of God.

The Word Changes Us.

What You
    Keep Seeing
You Will
    Eventually
Believe.

-MIKE MURDOCK

What Enters You Determines What Exits You.

-MIKE MURDOCK

31 REASONS YOU SHOULD READ THE WORD OF GOD DAILY

Daily Habits Create Permanent Changes.

**1.	The	Word	of	God Cleanses Your Character, Conduct And Conscience.** "Wherewithal shall a young man cleanse his way? by taking heed thereto according to Thy Word," (Psalm 119:9).

"Now ye are clean through the Word which I have spoken unto you," (John 15:3).

**2.	The Word of God Builds Your Faith.** "So then faith cometh by hearing, and hearing by the Word of God," (Romans 10:17).

**3.	The Word of God Imparts Power To Resist Sin.** "Thy Word have I hid in mine heart, that I might not sin against Thee," (Psalm 119:11).

4. The Word of God Is The Strength of God Within You. "My soul melteth for heaviness: strengthen Thou me according unto Thy Word," (Psalm 119:28). Each promise is like a time-release capsule...releasing energy, enthusiasm and Divine strength for the invisible, inner spirit within you.

5. The Word of God Will Stop Emotional Chaos And Devastation. "Unless Thy law had been my delights, I should have perished in mine affliction," (Psalm 119:92). It calms your nerves!

6. The Word of God Unleashes An Unexplainable Inner Joy. "The statutes of the Lord are right, *rejoicing* in the heart: the commandment of the Lord is pure, enlightening the eyes," (Psalm 19:8).

7. The Word of God Dramatically Strengthens Your Will Power To Do Right. "Thy Word have I hid in mine heart, that I might not sin against Thee," (Psalm 119:11).

8. The Word of God Provides Discernment In Your Decision-Making. "Thy Word is a lamp unto my feet, and a light unto my path," (Psalm 119:105).

9. The Word of God Clarifies Understanding of The Events And Happenings Around You. "The entrance of Thy words giveth light; it giveth understanding unto the simple," (Psalm 119:130).

10. The Word of God Gives Comfort During Stressful Times. "Remember the word unto Thy servant, upon which Thou hast caused me to hope. This is my comfort in my affliction: for Thy Word hath quickened me," (Psalm 119:49-50).

11. The Word of God Corrects Wrong Philosophies And Conclusions. "All scripture is given by inspiration of God, and is profitable for doctrine, for reproof, for correction, for instruction in righteousness," (2 Timothy 3:16).

12. The Word of God Purges Your Heart And Mind of Error, of Disastrous Consequences, of Wrong Choices. "The statutes of the Lord are right, rejoicing the heart: the commandment of the Lord is pure, enlightening the eyes," (Psalm 19:8).

13. The Word of God Gives Advance Warning. "Moreover by them is Thy servant warned: and in keeping of them there is great reward," (Psalm 19:11).

14. The Word of God Creates Moral Stability Within You And Prevents Backsliding. "The law of his God is in his heart; none of his steps shall slide," (Psalm 37:31).

15. The Word of God Gives Peace of Mind. "Great peace have they which love Thy law: and nothing shall offend them," (Psalm 119:165).

"And the work of righteousness shall be peace; and the effect of the righteousness quietness and assurance for ever," (Isaiah 32:17).

16. The Word of God Affects Your Health And Longevity of Life. "For length of days, and long life, *and peace,* shall they add to thee," (Proverbs 3:2).

17. The Word of God Establishes The Testimony of Weak People Who Became Strong. Look at Peter. He was a *pebble*...but became a foundation stone in the early church. A small stone. He became a great preacher on the Day of Pentecost.

Look at Zacchaeus. He climbed the tree to see Jesus. He was a thief, a liar, a cheat. Yet, God changed his life through his meeting with Jesus.

18. The Word of God Persuades You That A Wrong Person Can Become A Right Person. Look at the thief who asked Jesus to *remember* him "...when You come to Your kingdom." Calvary was not a loss...even on the same day it happened! Wrong people can become right people.

19. The Bible Is A Mentorship Program On How To Develop Your Personal Greatness. "Keep therefore and do them; for this is your Wisdom and your understanding in the sight of the nations, which shall hear all these statutes, and say, Surely this great nation is a wise and understanding people," (Deuteronomy 4:6).

20. The Word of God Shows You How Quickly God Can Turn You Into An Extraordinary Person. Saul put people in prison.

Yet, in one day God turned him into the great apostle Paul. *Miracles Happen As Quickly As Tragedies.*

21. The Bible Reveals The Secrets To Financial Prosperity And Breakthrough. It reveals the secret of creating a *supernatural* income *instantly.*

Read 1 Kings 17. The widow was broke, exhausted, bankrupt and starving. She was two pancakes away from starvation. Yet, the prophet shows up and motivates her to sow a Seed toward supply. The rest is history. "...and she and he, and her house, did eat many days." *The Bible documents the Miracle of Seed-Faith and how to make it work for you.*

22. The Word of God Shows You How Your Greatest Catastrophe Can Turn For Your Good In A Single Day. Look at Daniel in the lion's den...the laughing stock of those who were destroying him. Yet, God's protection brought him a promotion.

23. The Bible Is Your Handbook For Hope. "Remember the word unto Thy servant, upon which Thou hast caused me to hope," (Psalm 119:49). Job was a wealthy man who became an impoverished outcast. His relentless pursuit of Divine answers was honored by God. He recovered and became *twice* as blessed!

24. The Word of God Shows You The Incredible Miracle That Happens When You Hold On To Your Dream. Look at Joseph. His brothers sold him into slavery for $12.80. Yet, he held on to his dream. He became the Prime Minister of Egypt.

25. The Word of God Gives You Incredible Examples of How The Currents of Favor Can Take You From The Lowest Drudge of Society. Ruth was a peasant woman. A Moabite. She was taking care of her mother-in-law. Yet, through *the favor of God* with Boaz, became the wife of one of the wealthiest men in the entire area!

26. The Word of God Reveals How To Unleash The Miracle of Uncommon Favor In Your Life. "And Jesus increased in Wisdom and stature, and in favour with God and man," (Luke 2:52).

27. When You Read The Bible Aloud God Will Manifest His Presence. I do not really understand it, but it is a fact. As you begin to read His Words *aloud*, His Words pierce the atmosphere like Bells of Divine Anointing. A dead, silent and empty room can become charged with electricity within minutes as His Words are being spoken. I have seen it happen when I listen to the Bible spoken on cassette.

What is the importance of The Presence of God? Your views will *change* in His presence. Your perception is *corrected*. Your *faith* will *unleash* and explode in His presence. "...in Thy presence is fulness of joy; at Thy right hand there are pleasures for evermore," (Psalm 16:11).

28. The Word of God Changes The Focus of Your Mind. The Word exposes your mind to the *mentality* of God. Your heart is in the climate of *truth*. You are programming into your spirit *the very heart of God.*

29. The Word of God Is A

Barricade And Force In Preventing You From Entering The Lifestyle of A Rebel. It shows you the conclusion of a rebellious life. This is important. Pain *teaches*. Pain *motivates*. Pain *reveals*. *Pain is the birthplace of every significant change in your life.*

Many doctors have changed the lives of patients forever...by showing them photographs of what will happen if they do not make changes in their diet, eating habits and exercise.

God is merciful. He shows us what happens when men like Achan go against His instructions. He shows us what happens to women like Jezebel and men like King Ahab...who become obsessed with the possessions of others so much, they are willing to kill for them.

30. The Lives of Those Who Ignore His Word Often End In Disaster. What happens to people who ignore The Word of God, its laws and instructions? They have filled up the prisons, insane asylums and wards of hospitals where depression is as rampant as an epidemic.

31. The Word of God Is The First Instrument of Change The Holy Spirit Uses To Change You. First, it changes your *thoughts*...about *God*. Then, it changes your thoughts about *yourself*...your *enemy*...your *future*...your past *mistakes...eternity and death*...and your present *adversity*.

These are just a few of the many benefits. Without the continuous entrance of The Word, you will miss every Divine Reward planned for your life.

The workings of God in your life are *not* proportionate to your *need* of God. God works in your life proportionate to your *knowledge* of Him. (Read Hosea 4:6.)

Oh precious friend! Listen to me today! Launch out into the depths of The Word of God. Throw yourself toward The Word! Make it the first priority of every day.

The Word Is The Master Key To Change.

11 WISDOM KEYS TO HELP YOU BEGIN THIS GREAT HABIT

1. Quit Condemning Yourself And Carefully Begin Building The Bible Habit. Satan fights your reading the Bible more than any other habit because of the power you will develop as you read it. He will not oppose the reading of newspapers and novels. The opposition you feel as you attempt to read the Word is unseen, satanic, and devised to rob you of the Word's power and benefits. Once you develop the ability to at least begin reading each morning, The Holy Spirit reinforces that decision to act, and you will find yourself not wanting to quit!

2. Invest In A Quality Bible That Inspires You To Read It. Do you need large print? *Buy* the large print. Do you need a thin Bible that is easy to carry around? Then buy a *thin* Bible. Make any investment necessary...because it is the greatest book on earth.

3. Establish A Specific Place To Read Your Bible. God made places *before* He made people. When Elijah needed provision, God sent him to a place...the brook. When that place became empty and barren, God sent him to another place... Zarephath. God scheduled the birth of His Son *at a place.*

Sanctify that place. Make it "The Secret Place" where The Word of God is imparted into your life. It may be a recliner chair in the corner of your bedroom. It may be a desk in your den. You might want to designate an entire room...the place where you meet with God.

4. Keep A Daily Appointment With The Word. An *Appointment* shows the *importance* of the event. When you make an Appointment with your lawyer, it is big on your calendar. The family knows it. When you make an Appointment with your dentist, your boss even knows it. You take off work. You schedule your entire life around Appointments.

That is why it is important for you to have a Daily Appointment to read the Scriptures.

Choose a specific time to read The Word. It is easy to make a habit. Schedule a time that you can perpetuate, habitualize.

Attach it to something you *already* do regularly. Many read their Bible just before they go to bed... whatever time that is...every night. (The disadvantage is you are often too tired to respond appropriately at that time.) It really should be Priority #1...each morning.

5. Choose A System For Reading Your Bible. There are various systems and reading schedules for reading The Word of God.

Read it topically. That is, select a *specific* topic (for instance, The Holy Spirit) and begin to study that topic throughout The Word of God from Genesis to Revelation. Secure a Strong's Concordance and look up the appropriate and relating Scriptures.

Read Your Bible Progressively. When you read 3 chapters a day and 5 on Sunday, you will complete reading the Bible through its entirety within 12 months. When you read *9 chapters a day,* you will read the entire New Testament through within *30* days. When you read *40 chapters* a day, you will read the entire Bible *every month.*

Read Your Bible A Book At A Time. For example, take the small book of James and begin to read it daily over and over. It will astound you...what you begin to see in a book as you continue to gaze upon its truth...day after day. Some well-known men of God have been known to read a single book of the Bible, using this method, 20 or 30 times before reading any other part of the Bible.

What You See, You Will Do.

That is what is important about the Scriptures. What you see on those pages you will begin to do in every day life.

6. Read Great Amounts of The Scriptures. Someone said, "A cow must drink 3 gallons of water to produce one gallon of milk." Sometimes, you must absorb a lot of The Word...to keep it producing. You must learn it. Sometimes we want to sow a small Seed of The Word to produce an incredible Harvest. But, *Harvest is always proportionate to Seed sown.* "He which sowest sparingly shall reap also sparingly; and he which soweth bountifully shall reap also bountifully," (2 Corinthians 9:6).

7. Use Marking Pencils of Varied Colors. It adds *life* to your reading. You may want to use a *red* marking pencil for every Scripture concerning the *blood of Christ.* You may want to use *green* to mark *financial* Scriptures. Select your own system. (Use the kind of map pencils that do not bleed through thin paper.)

8. Memorize One Bible Verse A Day. Make it an appropriate verse for a *present need* in your life.

Example: If your Assignment is soul winning, memorize the Scriptures relating to winning souls to Christ.

9. Keep A Daily Wisdom Journal. Record impressions and

revelations. You will build a great *Wisdom Bank* of research material to review, reflect upon and retrieve for mentoring others. What a magnificent legacy to leave your children.

10. Become An Expert On One Specific Topic In The Bible. Memorize 31 Scriptures on your choice of subjects...faith, power, healing or salvation. *Whatever You Master, You Can Impart To Others.*

11. Begin Your Success Habit Today. You will not "wake up" to an easier time. Start *this very day.* Talk to others about the truths you have read *today.* Do not become frustrated attempting to remember it all. It will come back to you when necessary.

Just get into The Word, and The Word will get into you. You might keep a daily schedule.

Your attachment to The Word of God affects your attitude, your happiness and your achievements.

❧ 5 ❧

31 WISDOM KEYS TO CHANGE YOUR LIFE

1. Never Complain About What You Permit.
2. When Your Heart Decides The Destination, Your Mind Will Design The Map To Reach It.
3. The Proof of Desire Is Pursuit.
4. What You Respect, You Will Attract.
5. The Secret of Your Future Is Hidden In Your Daily Routine.
6. The Problem That Infuriates You The Most Is The Problem God Has Assigned You To Solve.
7. The Size of Your Enemy Determines The Size of Your Rewards.
8. What You Make Happen For Others, God Will Make Happen For You.
9. If You Insist On Taking Something God Did Not Give You, He Will Take Back Something He Gave You.

10. An Uncommon Seed Always Creates An Uncommon Harvest.
11. What You Can Tolerate, You Cannot Change.
12. Any Movement Toward Order Will Expose What Does Not Belong In Your Life.
13. Your Rewards In Life Are Determined By The Kinds of Problems You Are Willing To Solve For Others.
14. The Atmosphere You Create Determines The Product You Produce.
15. What You See Determines What You Desire.
16. Your Respect For Time Is A Prediction of Your Financial Future.
17. God Never Responds To Pain, But He Always Responds To Pursuit.
18. Greatness Is Not The Absence of A Flaw—But The Willingness To Overcome It.
19. One Day of Favor Is Worth A Thousand Days of Labor.
20. The Anointing You Respect Is The Anointing That Increases In

Your Life.

21. Those Who Sin With You Eventually Sin Against You.

22. When You Want Something You Have Never Had, You Must Do Something You Have Never Done.

23. The Proof of Love Is The Investment of Time.

24. What You Are Willing To Walk Away From Determines What God Will Bring To You.

25. What You Fail To Destroy Will Eventually Destroy You.

26. What You Hear Determines What You See.

27. What You Love Will Eventually Reward You.

28. What You Permit To Enter Your Life Will Determine What Exits Your Life.

29. What You Repeatedly Hear, You Eventually Believe.

30. What You Have In Your Hand Will Create Whatever You Want In Your Future.

31. False Accusation Is The Last Season Before Supernatural Promotion.

~ 6 ~
YOUR READ-THE-BIBLE THROUGH ONE YEAR PROGRAM SCHEDULE

JANUARY

1. Gen. 1-3	9. Gen. 27-29	17. Ex. 3-5	25. Ex. 29-33
2. Gen. 4-6	10. Gen. 30-32	18. Ex. 6-10	26. Ex. 34-36
3. Gen. 7-9	11. Gen. 33-37	19. Ex. 11-13	27. Ex. 37-39
4. Gen. 10-14	12. Gen. 38-40	20. Ex. 14-16	28. Ex. 40- Lev. 2
5. Gen. 15-17	13. Gen. 41-43	21. Ex. 17-19	29. Lev. 3-5
6. Gen. 18-20	14. Gen. 44-46	22. Ex. 20-22	30. Lev. 6-8
7. Gen. 21-23	15. Gen. 47-49	23. Ex. 23-25	31. Lev. 9-11
8. Gen. 24-26	16. Gen. 50-Ex. 2	24. Ex. 26-28	

FEBRUARY

1. Lev. 12-16	9. Num. 13-15	17. Dt. 3-5	25. Dt. 29-31
2. Lev. 17-19	10. Num. 16-18	18. Dt. 6-10	26. Dt. 32-34
3. Lev. 20-22	11. Num. 19-21	19. Dt. 11-13	27. Josh. 1-3
4. Lev. 23-25	12. Num. 22-24	20. Dt. 14-16	28. Josh. 4-6
5. Lev. 26-27-Num. 1	13. Num. 25-27	21. Dt. 17-19	
6. Num. 2-4	14. Num. 28-30	22. Dt. 20-22	
7. Num. 5-7	15. Num. 31-35	23. Dt. 23-25	
8. Num. 8-12	16. Num. 36-Dt. 2	24. Dt. 26-28	

MARCH

1. Josh. 7-11	9. Jud. 11-13	17. 1 Sam. 12-14	25. 2 Sam. 7-9
2. Josh. 12-14	10. Jud. 14-16	18. 1 Sam. 15-17	26. 2 Sam. 10-12
3. Josh. 15-17	11. Jud. 17-19	19. 1 Sam. 18-20	27. 2 Sam. 13-15
4. Josh. 18-20	12. Jud. 20-Ruth 1	20. 1 Sam. 21-23	28. 2 Sam. 16-18
5. Josh. 21-23	13. Ruth 2-4	21. 1 Sam. 24-26	29. 2 Sam. 19-23
6. Josh. 24-Jud. 2	14. 1 Sam. 1-3	22. 1 Sam. 27-31	30. 2 Sam. 24-1 Ki.
7. Jud. 3-5	15. 1 Sam. 4-8	23. 2 Sam. 1-3	31. 1 Ki. 3-5
8. Jud. 6-10	16. 1 Sam. 9-11	24. 2 Sam. 4-6	

APRIL

1. 1 Ki. 6-8	9. 2 Ki. 10-12	17. 1 Chr. 11-13	25. 2 Chr. 8-10
2. 1 Ki. 9-11	10. 2 Ki. 13-15	18. 1 Chr. 14-16	26. 2 Chr. 11-15
3. 1 Ki. 12-14	11. 2 Ki. 16-18	19. 1 Chr. 17-21	27. 2 Chr. 16-18
4. 1 Ki. 15-17	12. 2 Ki. 19-23	20. 1 Chr. 22-24	28. 2 Chr. 19-21
5. 1 Ki. 18-22	13. 2 Ki. 24-1 Chr. 1	21. 1 Chr. 25-27	29. 2 Chr. 22-24
6. 2 Ki. 1-3	14. 1 Chr. 2-4	22. 1 Chr. 28-2 Chr. 1	30. 2 Chr. 25-27
7. 2 Ki. 4-6	15. 1 Chr. 5-7	23. 2 Chr. 2-4	
8. 2 Ki. 7-9	16. 1 Chr. 8-10	24. 2 Chr. 5-7	

MAY

1. 2 Chr. 28-30	9. Neh. 8-10	17. Job 11-15	25. Job 39-41
2. 2 Chr. 31-33	10. Neh. 11-Est. 2	18. Job 16-18	26. Job 42-Ps. 2
3. 2 Chr. 34-Ez. 2	11. Est. 3-5	19. Job 19-21	27. Ps. 3-5
4. Ez. 3-5	12. Est. 6-8	20. Job 22-24	28. Ps. 6-8
5. Ez. 6-8	13. Est. 9-Job 1	21. Job 25-27	29. Ps. 9-11
6. Ez. 9-Neh. 1	14. Job 2-4	22. Job 28-30	30. Ps. 12-14
7. Neh. 2-4	15. Job 5-7	23. Job 31-33	31. Ps. 15-19
8. Neh. 5-7	16. Job 8-10	24. Job 34-38	

JUNE

1. Ps. 20-22	9. Ps. 46-48	17. Ps. 72-74	25. Ps. 98-100
2. Ps. 23-25	10. Ps. 49-51	18. Ps. 75-77	26. Ps. 101-103
3. Ps. 26-28	11. Ps. 52-54	19. Ps. 78-80	27. Ps. 104-106
4. Ps. 29-31	12. Ps. 55-57	20. Ps. 81-83	28. Ps. 107-111
5. Ps. 32-34	13. Ps. 58-60	21. Ps. 84-88	29. Ps. 112-114
6. Ps. 35-37	14. Ps. 61-65	22. Ps. 89-91	30. Ps. 115-117
7. Ps. 38-42	15. Ps. 66-68	23. Ps. 92-94	
8. Ps. 43-45	16. Ps. 69-71	24. Ps. 95-97	

JULY

1. Ps. 118-120	9. Ps. 144-146	17. Pro. 20-22	25. SoS. 3-5
2. Ps. 121-123	10. Ps. 147-149	18. Pro. 23-25	26. SoS. 6-Is. 2
3. Ps. 124-126	11. Ps. 150-Pro. 2	19. Pro. 26-30	27. Is. 3-5
4. Ps. 127-129	12. Pro. 3-7	20. Pro. 31-Ecc. 2	28. Is. 6-8
5. Ps. 130-134	13. Pro 8-10	21. Ecc. 3-5	29. Is. 9-11
6. Ps. 135-137	14. Pro. 11-13	22. Ecc. 6-8	30. Is. 12-14
7. Ps. 138-140	15. Pro. 14-16	23. Ecc. 9-11	31. Is. 15-17
8. Ps. 141-143	16. Pro. 17-19	24. Ecc. 12-SoS. 2	

AUGUST

1. Is. 18-20	9. Is. 44-48	17. Jer. 6-8	25. Jer. 32-34
2. Is. 21-25	10. Is. 49-51	18. Jer. 9-11	26. Jer. 35-37
3. Is. 26-28	11. Is. 52-54	19. Jer. 12-14	27. Jer. 38-40
4. Is. 29-31	12. Is. 55-57	20. Jer. 15-17	28. Jer. 41-43
5. Is. 32-34	13. Is. 58-60	21. Jer. 18-20	29. Jer. 44-46
6. Is. 35-37	14. Is. 61-63	22. Jer. 21-23	30. Jer. 47-51
7. Is. 38-40	15. Is. 64-66	23. Jer. 24-28	31. Jer. 52-Lam. 2
8. Is. 41-43	16. Jer. 1-5	24. Jer. 29-31	

SEPTEMBER

1. Lam. 3-5	9. Ez. 24-26	17. Dan. 2-4	25. Joel 2-Amos
2. Ez. 1-3	10. Ez. 27-29	18. Dan. 5-7	26. Amos 2-6
3. Ez. 4-6	11. Ez. 30-32	19. Dan. 8-10	27. Amos 7-9
4. Ez. 7-9	12. Ez. 33-35	20. Dan. 11-Hos. 3	28. Ob. 1-Jon. 2
5. Ez. 10-12	13. Ez. 36-40	21. Hos. 4-6	29. Jon. 3-Mi. 1
6. Ez. 13-17	14. Ez. 41-43	22. Hos. 7-9	30. Mi. 2-4
7. Ez. 18-20	15. Ez. 44-46	23. Hos. 10-12	
8. Ez. 21-23	16. Ez. 47-Dan. 1	24. Hos. 13-Joel 1	

OCTOBER

1. Mi. 5-7	9. Zech. 13-	16. Matt. 18-20	24. Mk. 16-Lk. 2
2. Na. 1-3	Mal. 1	17. Matt. 21-23	25. Lk. 3-7
3. Hab. 1-3	10. Mal. 2-4	18. Matt. 24-28	26. Lk. 8-10
4. Zeph. 1-Hag. 2	11. Matt. 1-5	19. Mk. 1-3	27. Lk. 11-13
5. Zech. 1-3	12. Matt. 6-8	20. Mk. 4-6	28. Lk. 14-16
6. Zech. 4-6	13. Matt. 9-11	21. Mk. 7-9	29. Lk. 17-19
7. Zech. 7-9	14. Matt. 12-14	22. Mk. 10-12	30. Lk. 20-22
8. Zech. 10-12	15. Matt. 15-17	23. Mk. 13-15	31. Lk. 23-Jn. 1

NOVEMBER

1. Jn. 2-6	9. Acts 9-11	16. Rom. 4-6	24. 1 Cor. 14-16
2. Jn. 7-9	10. Acts 12-14	17. Rom. 7-9	25. 2 Cor. 1-3
3. Jn. 10-12	11. Acts 15-17	18. Rom. 10-12	26. 2 Cor. 4-6
4. Jn. 13-15	12. Acts 18-20	19. Rom. 13-15	27. 2 Cor. 7-9
5. Jn. 16-18	13. Acts 21-23	20. Rom. 16-1 Cor. 2	28. 2 Cor. 10-12
6. Jn. 19-21	14. Acts 24-26	21. 1 Cor. 3-5	29. 2 Cor. 13-
7. Acts 1-3	15. Acts 27-	22. 1 Cor. 6-10	Gal. 4
8. Acts 4-8	Rom. 3	23. 1 Cor. 11-13	30. Gal. 5-Eph. 1

DECEMBER

1. Eph. 2-4	8. 1 Tim. 3-5	16. James 2-4	24. Rev. 6-7
2. Eph. 5-Ph. 1	9. 1 Tim. 6-2 Tim. 2	17. James 5-1 Pet. 2	25. Rev. 8-9
3. Ph. 2-4	10. 2 Tim. 3-Ti. 1	18. 1 Peter 3-5	26. Rev. 10-11
4. Col. 1-3	11. Ti. 2-3-Phil. 1	19. 2 Peter 1-3	27. Rev. 12-16
5. Col. 4-	12. Heb. 1-3	20. 1 John 1-5	28. Rev. 17-18
1 Thes. 2	13. Heb. 4-6	21. 2 Jn. 1-3 Jn.-Jude 1	29. Rev. 19-20
6. 1 Thes. 3-2 Thes. 2	14. Heb. 7-11	22. Rev. 1-3	30. Rev. 21-22
7. 2 Thes. 3-1 Tim. 2	15. Heb. 12-James 1	23. Rev. 4-5	31. Well Done!

DECISION

Will You Accept Jesus As Your Personal Savior Today?

The Bible says, "That if thou shalt confess with thy mouth the Lord Jesus, and shalt believe in thine heart that God hath raised Him from the dead, thou shalt be saved," (Romans 10:9).

Pray this prayer from your heart today!

"Dear Jesus, I believe that You died for me and rose again on the third day. I confess I am a sinner...I need Your love and forgiveness...Come into my heart. Forgive my sins. I receive Your eternal life. Confirm Your love by giving me peace, joy and supernatural love for others. Amen."

❏ Yes, Mike, I made a decision to accept Christ as my personal Savior today. Please send me my free gift of your book *31 Keys To A New Beginning* to help me with my new life in Christ.

Name _____ Birthdate ___/___

Address _____

City _____ State_____ Zip _____

Phone (_____)_____ E-Mail _____

Mail To: DFC

The Wisdom Center · 4051 Denton Hwy. · Ft. Worth, TX 76117
1-817-759-BOOK · 1-817-759-2665 · 1-817-759-0300
You Will Love Our Website..! MikeMurdockBooks.com

Unless otherwise indicated, all Scripture quotations are taken from the King James Version of the Bible.
The Greatest Success Habit On Earth · ISBN 1-56394-029-9/B-80
Copyright © 1994 by **MIKE MURDOCK**
All publishing rights belong exclusively to Wisdom International
Publisher/Editor: Deborah Murdock Johnson
Published by The Wisdom Center · 4051 Denton Hwy. · Ft. Worth, TX 76117
1-817-759-BOOK · 1-817-759-2665 · 1-817-759-0300
You Will Love Our Website..! MikeMurdockBooks.com

Clip and Mail

31

■ Has embraced his Assignment to Pursue...Proclaim...and Publish the Wisdom of God to help people achieve their dreams and goals.

■ Began full-time evangelism at the age of 19, which has continued since 1966.

■ Has traveled and spoken to more than 23,000 audiences in over 200 countries, including East and West Africa, Asia and Europe.

■ Noted author of over 600 books, including best sellers, *Wisdom For Winning, Dream Seeds* and *The Double Diamond Principle*.

■ Created the popular *Topical Bible* series for Businessmen, Mothers, Fathers, Teenagers; *The One-Minute Pocket Bible* series and *The Uncommon Life* series.

■ Has composed more than 5,700 songs such as "I Am Blessed," "You Can Make It," "God Rides On Wings of Love" and "Jesus, Just The Mention of Your Name," recorded by many gospel artists.

■ Is the Founder of The Wisdom Center, in Ft. Worth, Texas.

■ Has a weekly television program called *Wisdom Keys With Mike Murdock*.

■ Has appeared often on TBN, CBN, BET and other television network programs.

■ The Creator of The Master 7 Mentorship System.

■ Has led over 3,000 to accept the call into full-time ministry.

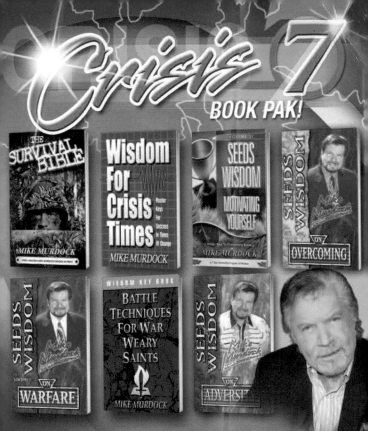

Crisis 7 BOOK PAK!

❶ The Survival Bible (Book/B-29/248pg/$12)

❷ Wisdom For Crisis Times (Book/B-40/112pg/$9)

❸ Seeds of Wisdom on Motivating Yourself (Book/B-171/32pg/$5)

❹ Seeds of Wisdom on Overcoming (Book/B-17/32pg/$5)

❺ Seeds of Wisdom on Warfare (Book/B-19/32pg/$5)

❻ Battle Techniques For War Weary Saints (Book/B-07/32pg/$5)

❼ Seeds of Wisdom on Adversity (Book/B-21/32pg/$5)

*Each Wisdom Book may be purchased separately if so desired.

DR. MIKE MURDOCK

The Wisdom Center
Crisis 7
Book Pak!
Only $30 $46
Value
WBL-25
Wisdom Is The Principal Thing

Add 20% For S/H

THE WISDOM CENTER
4051 Denton Highway • Fort Worth, TX 76117

1-817-759-BOOK
1-817-759-0300

You Will Love Our Website...!
MikeMurdockBooks.com

Money 7
BOOK PAK!

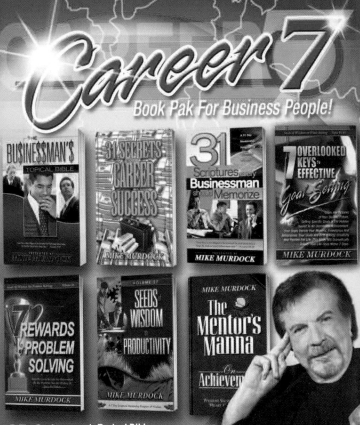

Career 7
Book Pak For Business People!

DR. MIKE MURDOCK

❶ **The Businessman's Topical Bible** (Book/B-33/384pg/$10)

❷ **31 Secrets for Career Success** (Book/B-44/114pg/$12)

❸ **31 Scriptures Every Businessman Should Memorize** (Book/B-141/32pg/$5)

❹ **7 Overlooked Keys To Effective Goal-Setting** (Book/B-127/32pg/$7)

❺ **7 Rewards of Problem Solving** (Book/B-118/32pg/$7)

❻ **Seeds of Wisdom on Productivity** (Book/B-137/32pg/$7)

❼ **The Mentor's Manna on Achievement** (Book/B-79/32pg/$5)

Each Wisdom Book may be purchased separately if so desired.

The Wisdom Center
Career 7 Book Pak!
Only $30 $53 Value
WBL-27
Wisdom Is The Principal Thing

Add 20% For S/H

The Wisdom Papers of Mike Murdock

30 Different Wisdom Papers For Only $10..!

1. *7 Keys To Motivating Yourself!* (WPMM#1PK)
2. *7 Qualities of An Uncommon Leader* (WPMM#2PK)
3. *Guidance* (WPMM#3PK)
4. *When You're Tired of Waiting For A Miracle!* (WPMM#4PK)
5. *12 Facts You Should Know About Wisdom!* (WPMM#5PK)
6. *7 Things You Need To Know To Become A Millionaire* (WPMM#6PK)
7. *15 Facts About Miracles* (WPMM#7PK)
8. *20 Ways To Improve Your Relationships* (WPMM#8PK)
9. *The Master Key To Achieving Your Dream..!* (WPMM#9PK)
10. *Expectation* (WPMM#10PK)
11. *14 Keys To Managing Your Mind* (WPMM#11PK)
12. *Greatness...The Disguised Treasure* (WPMM#12PK)
13. *The Uncommon Dream* (WPMM#13PK)
14. *Nurture Relationships Connected To Your Dream* (WPMM#14PK)
15. *The Seed of Submission* (WPMM#15PK)
16. *Surviving Your Season of Testing* (WPMM#16PK)
17. *Unlock Your Miracle...For Your Uncommon Dream* (WPMM#17PK)
18. *Prosperity...And 3 Scriptural Reasons You Should Pursue It* (WPMM#18PK)
19. *Territorial Order* (WPMM#19PK)
20. *Loneliness, Love And The Christian Single* (WPMM#20PK)
21. *How To Delegate Effectively* (WPMM#21PK)
22. *Dealing With An Enemy...18 Facts You Must Never Forget..!* (WPMM#22PK)
23. *Peace Is Not The Absence of Conflict...It Is The Absence of Inner Conflict* (WPMM#23PK)
24. *Your Assignment Will Always Be To Someone Who Is Hurting* (WPMM#24PK)
25. *The Financial Crisis And The Believer* (WPMM#25PK)
26. *The Unhappy Voices Around You* (WPMM#26PK)
27. *Are You Nurturing A Strength or A Weakness?* (WPMM#27PK)
28. *10 Master Keys For Parents And Teachers* (WPMM#28PK)
29. *Passion: The Secret Weapon* (WPMM#29PK)
30. *Move Toward The Voice of The Holy Spirit..!* (WPMM#30PK)

The Wisdom Center
30 Titles
ONLY $10..!
add $2.00 S/H
WPMM 1-30 PK
Wisdom Is The Principal Thing

THE WISDOM CENTER
4051 Denton Highway • Fort Worth, TX 76117

1-817-759-BOOK
1-817-759-0300

You Will Love Our Website...!
MikeMurdockBooks.com

14 Harvests Are Waiting For You..!

Dear Friend,

God has connected us!

I have asked The Holy Spirit for 3000 Special Partners who will plant a monthly Seed of $58.00 to help me bring the gospel around the world. (58 represents 58 kinds of blessings in the Bible.)

Will you become my monthly Faith Partner in The Wisdom Key 3000? Your monthly Seed of $58.00 is so powerful in helping heal broken lives. When you sow into the work of God, 4 Miracle Harvests are guaranteed in Scripture, Isaiah 58...

▶ Uncommon Health (Isaiah 58)
▶ Uncommon Wisdom For Decision-Making (Isaiah 58)
▶ Uncommon Financial Favor (Isaiah 58)
▶ Uncommon Family Restoration (Isaiah 58)

I would love to hear from you. Email me today at
DrMurdock@TheWisdomCenter.tv..!

Your Faith Partner,

Mike Murdock

P.S. Will You Become My Ministry
Partner In The Work of God?

PP-03
